# Beautiful Napkin Folding

# Beautiful Napkin Folding

## HORST HANISCH

Sterling Publishing Co., Inc.
New York

# Table of Contents

Library of Congress Cataloging-in-Publication Data Available

10 9 8 7 6 5 4 3 2 1

First paperback edition published in 2002 by
Sterling Publishing Company, Inc.
387 Park Avenue South, New York, N.Y. 10016
First published in Germany by Falken Verlag
under the title *Servieten Formen*
© 1999 by Falken Verlag
English translation © 2000 by Sterling Publishing
Company, Inc.
Distributed in Canada by Sterling Publishing
C/o Canadian Manda Group, One Atlantic Avenue, Suite 105
Toronto, Ontario, Canada M6K 3E7
Distributed in Australia by Capricorn Link (Australia) Pty Ltd.
P.O. Box 704, Windsor, NSW 2756 Australia

*Printed in China*

Sterling  ISBN 0-8069-6831-1  Hardcover
         ISBN 1-4027-0071-7  Paperback

*The napkin, today taken for granted in every well-run household, is a relatively recent invention. For quite a while, it was an important requisite only at the table of the upper classes. In the meantime, it has acquired its secure place in all strata of society. The increased interest in this very helpful piece of table culture is due to the fact that today, its decorative value is being recognized. The trend is definitely moving in the direction of imaginatively shaped figures of serviettes.*

▷ *In "The Breakfast of the Oarsmen," painted in 1881 by Renoir, people eating breakfast have gathered casually on a terrace.*

# A Brief Word About Napkins

The nice custom of covering the dining table with a linen cloth originated in medieval times. Old pictures show that table cloths then reached down to the floor — a practical feature — thus one could use the overhanging part as a protection for clothing and, at the same time, one could use it to wipe the fingers and mouth.

**From tablecloth to napkin**
For thousands of years in every country, depending on the epoch, different cultures of dining developed.

▽ *During our grandmothers' generation, hand–embroidered cloth napkins were of course part of the dowry. The very precious items were well taken care of.*

Today, among different cultures and customs of eating and drinking, table manners as well as the use of napkins are quite varied. In medieval times, Europeans still used the large cloths covering the table for wiping their mouths and fingers.

About 300 years ago, when the napkin was introduced, the function of tablecloth and serviette were separated. But it was not until the 18th century that, especially in France, a real culture of

*▽ Dinner with a bourgeois family during the first half of the 19th century; colored copper engraving by Johann Michael Voltz. The master of the house has, as was the fashion then, fastened the large napkin at the top of his collar. Today, on the other hand, napkins are placed on one's lap.*

dining developed where the napkin had its firm place. At that time, the serviette was a purely decorative element; it could be large and splendid, while today, it is always used.

The decisive impetus for the refinement of table manners and customs came about when, in 1710, Count von Tschirmhaus and Johann Friedrich Böttger rediscovered porcelain. In 1719, the first porcelain manufacture was established. This was the time of the porcelain service set that had many pieces decorated in the same way. Furthermore, the opulent table setting was furnished aristocratically with beautiful silverware for both the serving of food and for decor. It comes as no surprise that, at the same time, artful and expansive shapes for napkins were developed. The

hosts, in fact, competed with one another in arranging this useful as well as decorative accessory on their festive banquet table. At the court of Emperor Franz Joseph I (1830–1916), the most expensive kind of damask napkins decorated with the woven coat of arms were used.

These napkins, according to the tradition of the imperial table were folded. Today, there is a renewal of such traditional forms.

◁ *"Dinner at the imperial court" (1895) The festive banquet table of Wilhelm II shown in a colored woodcut by William Pape. The ornamentation is made up of flowers and splendid table decorations.*

▽ *In the 1928 silent movie "The Ballet Elector" the table is set for dinner with delicate flowers and napkins lying flat. This is a scene with Dina Gralla and Albert Pauling; the still was colored later.*

### When grandfather married grandmother

People in our grandparents' generation owned very beautiful cloth napkins embroidered by hand with patterns and occasionally very large monograms. They were part of the dowry and were guarded as precious heirlooms. They are seldom used because it is difficult to clean and starch them.

Napkins were so well taken care of that they often survived many households. Today, people who store these napkins do not fold them but place them flat on top of each other so they do not incur unnecessary creases.

### The napkin in modern times

In our century, two world wars and their respective aftermaths resulted in the pre occupation with survival for most of the populace. The interest in the refined art of setting the table and the shapes of napkins, was, thus, accordingly small. Only after economic and social recovery after World War II, in the wake of the 1950's economic miracle, was there a renewed interest in opulently presented napkins.

*△ In the style of the thirties, tea was served in simple cups. The correct setting of the table was taught in home economics.*

### Cloth and paper napkins

In the seventies, many countries in the West developed a distinct consciousness for hygiene. At this point, the extremely practical paper napkins almost completely pushed aside the cloth napkins. In general, the napkin was not folded in any particular way but simply put down flat. For hygienic reasons, people usually consciously refrained from folding napkins.

### Manifold ways of shaping napkins

Before you begin shaping napkins, get an overview of what is currently available in the stores. Paper napkins are available today in every imaginable color and in the most varied of patterns — an important factor if you intend on setting accents with napkins. Just to get an idea of the hues available in the trade, some examples are: green, hunter's green, jade green, reed green, pink, rose–colored pink, dark pink, Bordeaux red, yellow, golden yellow, buttermilk yellow, melon, orange, sand, lilac, violet, light blue, blue, dark blue, charcoal grey, grey, white, silver, gold, and black.

### The renaissance of the art of the napkin

Let's take a brief look back at the history of the art of napkin folding. Originally, napkins were used mainly for decorative purposes. Today, once again, this function is being brought back. Napkins are being arranged artfully under bowls, vases, candle holders, and even flower arrangements. The use of napkins for decorative purposes offers boundless possibilities of configurations, especially in combination with other materials. People who enjoy the unusual can experiment with eye–catching fan–shaped napkins, or column-like figures, which will, when standing in the background on a sideboard or buffet, display their beautiful effect.

In 1981, I produced the first new napkins book because the change in dining behavior could not be overlooked. A beautifully set table created with a lot imagination in color and shape was valued once more and, of course, original napkins were part of it.

Today, the art of the shape of napkins is experiencing a renaissance. The little cloth for wiping one's mouth is no longer regarded as just a practical accessory. Its great decorative value is appreciated once more. Join countless others in creating the most beautiful forms.

◁ *"The Dinner" shows a bourgeois family, from a chalk lithography dating around 1860 (left page). Very large napkins protected clothing. For the children they were knotted in the back.*

▽ *"The Noon Meal in the Hot House," painted in 1877 by Louise Abbema. An upper middle class family dines in an exotic ambience.*

# All Around the Napkin

Personal style, individuality, and creativity are in demand on occasions where tables and banquet tables are set. Whether classic, elegant, original, or romantic, there are ideas and practical hints for every style and every occasion.

# Basic Considerations

*There are two kinds of napkins: napkins used to wipe one's mouth and the so-called "handling napkins." The first group includes the larger dinner napkin, the smaller cocktail napkin, and the decorative napkin. Also included in this group is, of course, the napkin used for wiping one's mouth, which is also used occasionally as a buffet napkin. All of these are used by the guest — though the decorative napkin will be used only to a certain degree. The napkins for serving food, on the other hand, are used by personnel in restaurants.*

▷ *Cloth napkins simple or with a woven pattern are available in large selections and many colors.*

Napkins for serving food are true working napkins. For use in the home, have a good dish towel either in a noble white color or with a nice decoration ready for use in the kitchen. It is not folded in any special way. On the other hand, with "handling napkins," let your imagination roam and shine with the most diverse figures. In this book, we will introduce many original ideas. Surprise guests each time anew.

Guest and host use the napkins to wipe their mouth during a meal and dab their lips with it afterwards.

The napkin is also used to protect clothing. At the beginning of a meal the napkin that is set up on the cover is taken off the table, unfolded, and put into your lap.

### Napkins on the table and on the buffet

Napkins are not necessarily arranged only on the festive table. There are several occasions when table napkins aren't arranged: 1) when planning a sumptuous decor of flowers that should get full attention; 2) at a summer meal when nothing should detract one's guests from the plates of cold food. On this type of occasion, napkins can be placed on the buffet or sideboard.

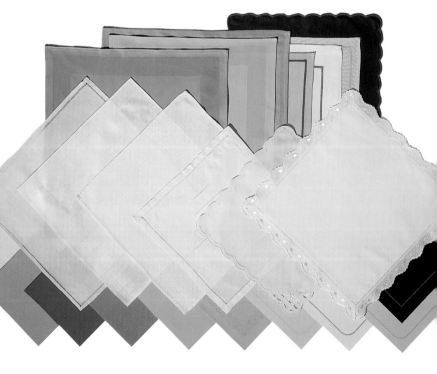

Your guests will then serve themselves and admire the gorgeous colors. Napkins displayed this way are also called buffet napkins.

Larger napkins for wiping one's mouth are appropriate when you are serving a festive meal with several courses, e.g. hors d'oeuvres, main course and dessert.

### Cocktail napkins

If there is a reception champagne and snacks will be served, guests will fare better with smaller cocktail napkins. They are offered in large varieties and are thinner than the usual napkins. They are never suitable for use at the table.

For the sake of decoration, one can distribute some charmingly arranged napkins on the banquet table as if they were candles or flowers.

Decorative napkins are most effective if they set a colorful accent as the main theme of an overall arrangement. Here, a single color, as well as a sophisticated color combination, can serve you. It's best to arrange color in reference to the rest of the table decoration and the service.

### Small tablecloth

For the sake of being complete I would like to briefly mention the small tablecloth (cover serviette). It has nothing to do with the napkin; it is rather a mini–tablecloth.

You will find this (usually around 80 x 80 cm) small tablecloth in good restaurants where it is placed over the actual, much larger tablecloth. It covers the area where stains usually occur. For every new customer, the table is covered with a fresh small tablecloth. It is not used in the privacy of the home.

### Paper napkin or cloth napkin?

In recent years, there has been a discussion as to whether preference should be given to the cloth or the paper napkin. Of course, both have their special advantages. Cloth napkins are often preferred because of their artful woven pattern or their decorations of pretty appliqués. On a

△ *People who own a large stock of napkins can create table decorations spontaneously.*

festively set table, they appear decidedly stylish and elegant. As for their practical side, they do show some important advantages: usually they are larger than paper napkins and protect clothing exceptionally well.

*△ Patterned napkins will provide interesting accents and can be combined with plain napkins.*

*▷ With a collection of napkins and decorative material, you will be able to set a table at any time according to your own ideas.*

Furthermore, they can be used over and over again, after the initial purchase. They are a low–cost solution. On the other hand, paper napkins are regarded as being especially hygienic. They are splendidly suitable for producing complicated napkin configurations because they always have the same format. Paper napkins never lose their shape, while cloth napkins eventually can. Furthermore, they do not cause additional work for the homemaker, because they don't need to be washed and ironed. Paper napkins come in all imaginable colors.

No matter which type of napkin one prefers, there is no problem giving an exquisite accent in the correct color to the table service or to the table decoration. In restaurants, as well as in the private home, the paper napkin is becoming more and more popular. The possibilities for decoration offered by the paper napkin are accommodating to the modern guest with his or her need for a sophisticated dining experience in refined surroundings.

Many paper napkins are currently being produced that are well suited for a combination with traditional linen, cloth, and table napkins. They can be combined without trouble. Often, because of the contrasting materials a special charm is created.

# Around the Set Table

*A festive meal is about mood setting. If one cares to offer it, one can create an ambiance that is the equal of the culinary delicacies on the table. Guests will rave about the meal for a long time to come. In order to create this feeling, take many things into consideration. After all, some fundamental knowledge is necessary to set the table stylishly and in accordance with the standard rules.*

For lovers of beautifully shaped napkins, the napkins will be the main attraction on the table. And for the main attraction to be in the limelight, the surroundings have to be just right. That means, first of all, you must think about everything that is part of a perfectly set table; then, you must organize all the elements of the arrangement. Relaxation should be a theme; a harmonious picture in regard to the table decoration will contribute substantially. Thus, one should see to it that the silverware is set absolutely parallel and at a right angle to the edge of the table. When shaping napkins, perfection is also needed. However, remember that personal style is important. The napkin should reflect the host.

This is not critical. It is important though to keep the harmonious overall impression that one can see when looking at the beautifully set tables in this book. In this book, in the photographs, it appears that only one place setting (at the bottom) is done correctly. But, it is simply an optical illusion due to the perspective when photographing.

### The cover

The cover, aside from the napkin, consists of silverware, plates, glasses, and pretty, decorative knife holders. Today, the knife holders are recognized as being important, after being ignored for so long. They are counted as part of the cover. The usual silverware consists of: a large knife, a large fork, a large spoon, a knife for hors d'oeuvres, a dessert spoon, a dessert fork, and a dessert knife. If one owns a complete set of silverware, and it is necessary, set a fish knife and a fish fork.

If meals consist solely of one course, there is only one knife, one fork, and one glass. In addition to the dining plate, which includes the soup cup and possibly a small plate for

▷ *A simple cover is also sufficient for barbecues and outdoor picnics. The shaped napkin is arranged behind the cover.*

◁ *The napkins lie to the right of the cover. Please make sure that there is sufficient space on the table. Otherwise, the napkin will be too close to the glasses. Under certain circumstances, that can become dangerous, and it looks terrible.*

▷ *The napkin is placed to the left of the bread plate. That, of course, is only possible if bread and butter are not supposed to be set out from the beginning. Otherwise, the small problem of space can be solved in a simple manner by shaping the napkins into small breadbaskets.*

◁ *The extended cover is called for if at least three courses will be served. Added to this are the glasses for the wines suited to the individual courses. Here, the napkins are on the dinner plate.*

▷ *To the left of the cover, this place offers itself if no bread plate is being set. Be sure the napkin of the neighboring cover is not getting too close and every guest knows right away which napkin belongs to his cover.*

bread. Today, frequently, a charger is put down to protect the table linen. More importantly, it functions as decoration because it will usually set a nice color accent. Glasses for red wine, white wine, and water should be set on the table. On special occasions, don't forget the champagne glasses. Aperitifs are likely to be served separately. Salt and pepper shakers are available as a set in both fancy and original design. These make all guests, who like things a bit more seasoned happy. Other spices are to be offered only with special foods. Mustard should be in a small mustard pot and with a little spoon. Ashtrays do not belong on the table.

All glasses are set in the right upper area of the cover. Knife and spoon lie on the right, with the exception of the bread knife and the dessert silverware. The forks — but not the dessert forks — are set on the left. All pieces of flatware on the left and right of the platter are used during hors d'oeuvres and main course. The flatware for dessert is placed at the top of the cover, the bread knife on the appropriate place for bread. The basic rule is: Silverware is always used from the outside to the inside, from top to bottom, and must be laid out in corresponding sequence. For hors d'oeuvres, two pieces of silverware are used at the same time. For soup and dessert only one piece of flatware is sufficient. The glass used during the hors d'oeuvres is set to the right and below the glass for the main course. To the top of these two glasses, there is a glass for the third drink.

*At a long table the napkins have to stand or lay in a perfect row and be in the same place at each cover.*

*On a round table too the covers have to be set accurately.*

### The napkin in the right place

There are many different possibilities when placing the napkin correctly on the cover. The following placing is common. On the dinner plate placed in the middle of the cover. Here, the coordination is always self-evident. If one has prepared a menu card, it is best placed between serviette and cover. By the way, this is an ideal solution for summer parties or for an evening on the terrace with a small circle of people. The "succession of courses" will thus be resistant to any gust of wind.

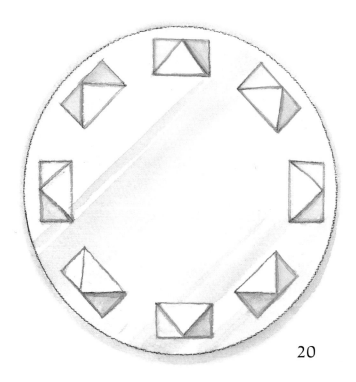

◁ *Napkins shaped as flat figures are usually placed on the plate because, otherwise, a very large table is needed.*

▷ *If the table is set in the same way but with different colors, a very different effect is achieved.*

◁ *If a napkin is placed at the top of the cover, the guest will have the greatest freedom of movement. But then the table has to have a certain width (depth).*

# Advanced Planning

*The last ten minutes before the guests arrive, the hand of the clock seems to race, the precious necklace has been misplaced, the guest list has vanished, and the candles do not want to burn at all. In order to avoid such chaos, everything should be planned in advanced, especially when hosting a large festive dinner party or if important guest are expected.*

Organization is the key — that is the motto if one wants to avoid stress during the last seconds. Then, the perfect host will receive his guests calmly and in the best of moods, which will then immediately transfer to the guests.

## Hints for preparation

The most important "working tool" one will need for a party is a check list that lists everything that needs to be done long before the important day arrives. It can be divided into groups: e.g., purchase of food, beverages, decoration, table linen, tableware, silverware etc. It can also be set up with respect to the proceedings in

time. Especially for preparations performed during the last minutes before the party starts, an exact list is very helpful. Do not forget, when planning to make a detailed seating chart and direct each guest to his place with the help of a place card. Thus, you'll ensure, with a bit of cleverness, that a harmonious grouping will result. Furthermore, this prevents guests from aimlessly milling around while last minute preparations are made. Enjoy the party before the start of the meal.

Now a small hint: Light the candles before the first bell rings. The wick is covered with wax and it takes a little while before it will start to burn really well. Usually hosts are somewhat nervous during the final preparations. All of the sudden, the heads of the matches will break off, or half burned heads of matches will fall on the tablecloth and disturbing spots will remain on it. Wicks that have been lit once before will relight very easily later on. Thus, the table will immediately radiate in festive brilliance without a hassle.

▷ *If you have a manifold collection of napkins and decorative material at your disposal, a very interesting table decor can be magically produced in a short time.*

### A *word about the napkins*

Here, too, lighten the burden for yourself a little. Though shapes for napkins are delicate works of art that can fall apart easily, there are some shapes which will keep their form longer and therefore can be prepared several days ahead of time. This way there will be time to fold them correctly. There will also be time to pursue other activities. On the following pages we have illustrated some classical figures for napkins that will survive a somewhat longer waiting period before their stage call. For sure, you will have encountered, several times before, these two classics of the art of folding napkins: the fan and the hat. When practicing, use a new napkin for each figure. If you use the same napkin several times, additional breaks and creases will be there and the following shapes cannot be formed at their best. The hat and fan are not easy to produce, but with a little practice one will certainly succeed. But if you are intent on having a favorite shape shine on the table, finish them ahead of time. If handled very carefully its shape will probably hold. The divided lines in the step–by–step drawings

△ *The unlimited variety of paper napkins available in the trade encourages more and more new creations.*

indicate that this napkin is folded over to the front. The point-lines show that the napkin is folded over to the back.

# Table Culture and the Use of Napkins

*Jean Anthelme Brillat-Savarin wrote in his frequently read book Physiology of Taste: "The joy of food we share with the animals, it only presupposes hunger and the necessities for its gratification. The joys of the table on the other hand are reserved for man only. They presuppose careful planning for the preparation of meals, the choice of place and the composition of guests."*

Not too long ago, table culture, a privilege of upper society, so to speak, gained importance for the bourgeoisie too. France, whose art of dining — in spite of the disappointments the modern traveler encounters there — was the precursor in this field.

The Early Victorian period, during the first half of the 19th century, reemphasized the importance of the domestic sphere and contributed to the refinement of table manners.

The round table was introduced, and social gatherings were cultivated where culinary pleasures were combined with the intellectual enjoyment of lively conversation in a cultured manner. The eyes, too, were given aesthetic enjoyment with the help of festive floral decor. Splendid flower arrangements in vases and gorgeous decor adorned the table. The Early Victorian flower bouquet, which is still treasured today, reminds us of this period when such charming decorations were very much valued. The understanding that a cultivated meal is not only good for life and soul but will also keep the family together, cement good friendships, and can be good

for business interests, enabled table culture flourish in the 19th and the beginning of the 20th century — thus the dinner speech became fashionable. In every solid middle–class home, a large service with many different pieces for various kinds of dishes were found and the lady of the house regarded it as a matter of honor to appealingly set the table with artfully folded napkins.

During the course of the 20th century, the self–absorption of the bourgeoisie came to an end. The structures of society were changed incisively; after World War II there remained hardly any time for banqueting. Fastfood restaurants sprung up and the both famous and infamous fast food saves a lot of work for people in the work force. Nevertheless, a remembrance of the comfortable round table with cultivated food cannot be overlooked. Once again, people enjoy cooking traditional solid dishes and eating refined food from all over the world, and increasing value is placed upon a corresponding ambience with fitting table decor as well as ever newly presented serviettes as an expression of a special dining culture.

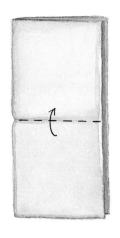

◁ △ *Fold your napkin lightly if you briefly leaves the table during the meal.*

### A small Emily Post guide to napkins

Of course, table manners suffered a bit in the meantime; especially the correct handling of napkins, which is no longer common knowledge for everyone. In many families, however, it is still a tradition to keep a napkin ready for use for each family member in a napkin ring marked with a name. Another fine custom that can still be encountered occasionally is to put the napkin in its own finely embroidered napkin bag.

But what to do with napkins during meals, and where does one put them? After a guest has sat down, first he will start a conversation with his neighbor at the table and enjoy his aperitif if it is being offered. As soon as wine has been served and thus the festive meal is underway, the guest takes the napkin unfolds it

and puts it in his lap to protect his clothing from food or drink that might possibly spill on him. The napkin does not belong in front of the tie, behind the shirt button, or into the decolleté. First of all, that will disturb the picture of a formal gathering. Secondly it gives the impression of being unable to eat in a cultured manner and with the necessary restraint. That a

napkin cannot be left unused on the cover because it is shaped so nicely is self–evident.

During dinner the napkin is placed in your lap. Once in a while lift it off daintily at the edge to dab your mouth. This is mandatory before reaching for a glass because otherwise your mouth could leave very visible grease marks. When the festive meal has ended, place the napkin lightly rolled together or folded on the table at your place. If, during the meal, you leave the table, the napkin is to be deposited lightly folded with the used side on the inside, on your chair.

◁ *If you leave the table during the meal the napkin is placed on your chair.*

# Shaping Napkins

Looking for an appropriate napkin shape for the Easter or Christmas table? Something original for a child's birthday? Do you have guests from Sweden, Spain, or Japan? Are you planning an elegant dinner or a garden party? In this large selection, you will find shapes of napkin for every occasion — reproducible with the help of step–by–step instructions.

# Love Letter

*Who does not like to receive a letter that comes from the heart? As a small favor for an especially nice guest, simply stick in a small surprise.*

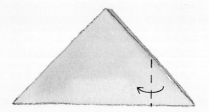

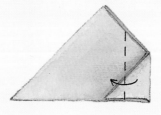

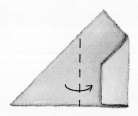

1. Fold the napkin at one of the diagonals to make a triangle. Fold over the right corner towards the middle.

2. Fold over the right corner towards the middle.

3. Fold the left corner so far to the right that the folded edge is symmetrical to the fold on the right.

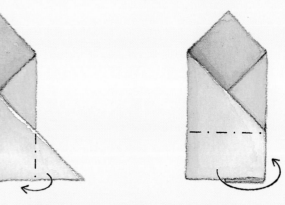

4. Fold overlapping edges to the back.

5. Fold the lower third of the figure to the back.

# Small Parcel

*Do your guests want to depart already? Give them a small farewell present for the road wrapped in an artfully folded napkin.*

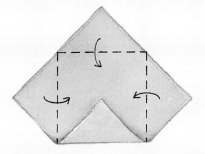

1. Fold the four corners of the napkin towards the middle.

2. Turn the napkin over.

3. Fold all three corners over to the middle.

4. Turn the figure over.

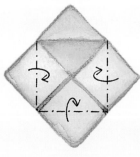

5. Enfold all four corners towards the inside.

# Small Breadbasket

*The crisp breakfast roll will really tempt your guest wrapped in this colorful figure.*
*It is very effective on the bread plate too.*

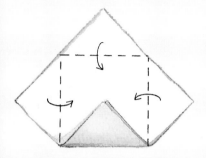

1. Place white napkin on gold napkin. Fold all corners towards the middle.

2. Turn the figure over.

3. Fold all corners towards the middle. Slide white napkin into gold napkin and fold to the top.

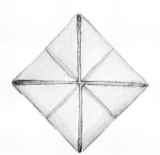

4. Fold all corners towards the inside.

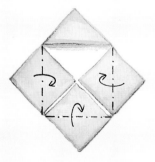

5. Slightly widen the four corners.

31

# Domino Fans

*Depending on your focal point, the look of the table setting will vary if it is embellished with domino fans. When looking at it from the front, the dark color dominates; when looking from the back, a light color dominates.*

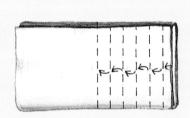

1. Fold the dark napkin over the light one.

2. Starting at the right, continuing to the middle, fold in accordion pleats.

3. Fold the figure in the middle towards the top.

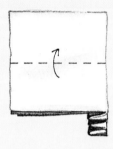

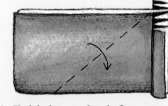

4. Fold down the left part towards the bottom.

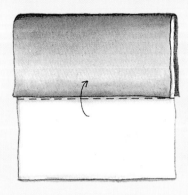

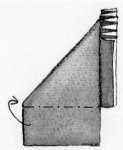

5. Tuck the overhanging part as a support behind the napkin.

*Classic*

# Festive Peak

*A classic among the art of the napkins — the festive peak with three corners. It
is folded quickly and fits excellently on an elegant table.*

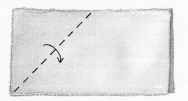

1. Fold the napkin in the
middle to make a triangle.
Fold the left upper corner
toward the middle.

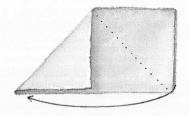

2. Pull down the right front
edge to the corner on the left.

3. Fold the right corner over
the left corner.

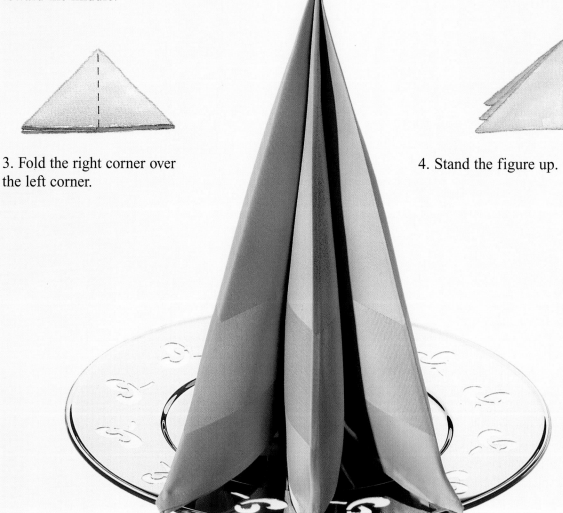

4. Stand the figure up.

# Sydney

*This unusual shape symbolizes the opera in Sydney, Australia - ideal if you are inviting guests who are enthusiastic about culture.*

1. Place white napkin on an apricot–colored napkin and fold to a triangle. Fold the triangle in the middle towards the top.

2. Fold over the left corner towards the front.

3. Fold over the right corner towards the front. Turn the figure over.

4. Fold over the left and right corners towards the front.

5. Pull out corners under the left and right edges. Turn over the napkin.

6. Grab the upper layer of the napkin at the top edge and pull up. Pull the second, third, and fourth layers at the top edge and pull towards the top.

# Two–Colored Hat

*This figure is seldom seen, but it is excellently suited for every festive table
where there is a lack of space. The two-colored hat will
also look very good in a glass.*

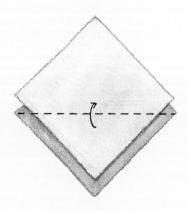

1. Place a light blue napkin on top of a dark blue one so that a dark blue edge will show. Fold the middle of the dark blue napkin towards the top.

2. Fold the lower edge to the top. Turn over the napkin.

3. Fold the left edge at the right.

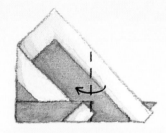

4. Fold the right edge to the left and, in the back, tuck under the edge that has been folded already.

5. Fold the overhanging edges to the inside.

# Striped Tower

*A napkin like an Egyptian tower: slender and ending in a peak.*
*Guests will be delighted.*

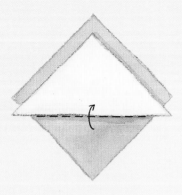

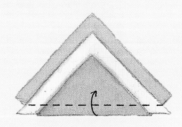

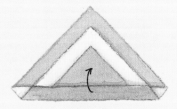

1. Fold the yellow napkin diagonally and place it on the green napkin. Fold up the lower green part.

2. Fold up parallel to the lower line.

3. Fold up the lower edge towards the top.

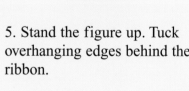

4. Turn napkin over. Starting at the right corner, roll in the napkin.

5. Stand the figure up. Tuck overhanging edges behind the ribbon.

# Lady's Shoe

*This shoe one can wear confidently — as an extravagant table decoration, of course.*

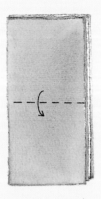

1. Place a white napkin on an apricot–colored napkin. Fold in half. Then fold over again to get a square shape.

2. Fold the corner of the apricot napkin upwards at the diagonal line.

3. Fold the corners of the two white layers upwards so that the apricot–colored edges will remain visible.

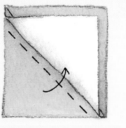

4. Fold the two apricot layers upwards so that a white edge remains.

5. Continue to fold the two white layers up towards the top.

6. Fold the last apricot–colored layer upwards. Then, turn the figure left at a 45° angle.

7. Turn the figure over . Fold the left corner upwards.

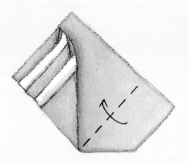

8. Fold the right corner upwards.

9. Turn the figure.

10. Arch the figure upwards on the vertical axis.

# Bridal Train

*The bride and groom are asking for the pleasure of your company. This is an extravagant figure for the wedding banquet.*

1. Fold the napkin diagonally upwards. Fold the right corner upwards.

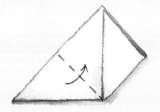

2. Fold the left corner upwards.

3. Turn the napkin over and fold in half.

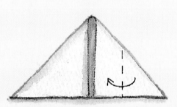

4. Fold the right corner towards the middle.

5. Fold the left corner to the middle and tuck under the tip of the right corner of the napkin.

6. Turn the figure around.

7. Pull to the right and left of the tips pointing upward. Stand the figure up.

# A Junk in Pink and Lavender

*Exotic charm from China, very much true to style with napkins in the shape of a junk. Savor and dream about the big wide world.*

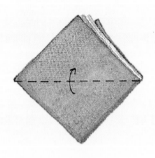

1. Place pink napkin on top of lavender–colored napkin and fold in half. Then fold in half to make a square.

2. Fold into a triangle.

3. Fold left corner diagonally into the front.

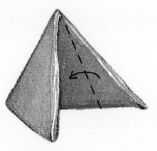

4. Fold the right corner into the front.

5. Fold both tips underneath the napkins.

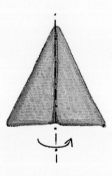

6. From the middle of the napkin, fold it in half, towards the back.

7. Push figure together at the lower left side.

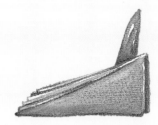

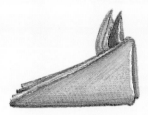

8. Stand the figure up.

9. Pull up the lavender colored tip on the top as the first sail.

10. Pull up the following pink tip. Pull up the other tips to get sails.

# Potatoes in Foil

*Whether with fresh rolls in the morning or rustic baked potatoes in the evening, these nicely shaped napkins keep both warm for a little while.*

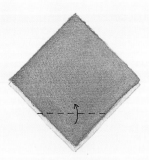

1. Place a blue napkin on a light yellow one. Fold the lower corner towards the middle.

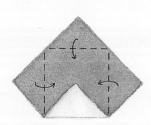

2. Fold all corners towards the middle.

3. Turn the figure around.

4. Fold the left upper corner towards the middle.

5. Fold the remaining corners towards the middle.

6. Turn the figure around.

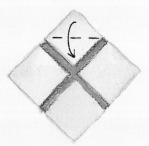

7. Fold the upper corner towards the middle.

8. Fold the remaining corners towards the middle.

9. Turn the figure around.

 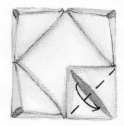

10. Turn the middle right and left corners out.

11. Turn the remaining middle corners out.

# Sea Urchin

*This figure presents itself exotically like the bizarre-looking animal of the sea.*
*It looks complicated but can be produced with ease.*

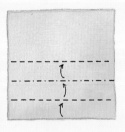

1. Fold the napkin into thirds. Then, fold in half. The bottom of the upper layer should be open.

2. Fold each pleat down, as shown in the illustration.

3. Fold the left third of the figure to the right.

4. Fold one half of the same part backwards.

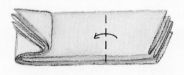

5. On the right, turn one third of the napkin to the left.

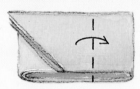

6. Fold half of that same part backwards.

7. Pull the corners lying on top towards the middle.

*Classic*

# Dove of Peace

*This figure presents itself harmoniously and peacefully. Perhaps one could place a small branch between its wings.*

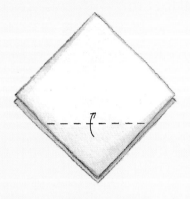

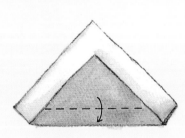

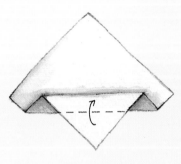

1. Place a white napkin on top of a lilac–colored napkin. Fold the lower corner up as shown.

2. Fold the triangle over the bottom.

3. Fold the triangle back up.

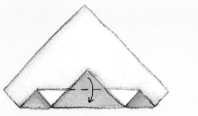

4. Fold the triangle down one more time.

5. Fold the top of the napkin down as shown.

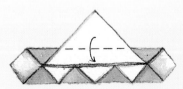

6. Fold the triangle back up.

7. Fold the upper triangle back down.

8. Fold the triangle back up.

9. Turn over the napkin. Fold the bottom triangle to the top triangle.

# Blooming Lily

*The delicate beauty and elegance of this regal flower is captured in this napkin figure. In its calix is even room for a small surprise.*

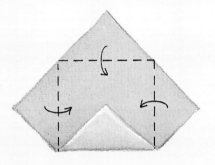

1. Place napkin in a diamond as shown. Fold each corner in towards the middle.

2. The napkin should now look like a square. Turn napkin so that it looks like a diamond.

3. Fold the right, left, and lower corners to the middle of the napkin.

4. Turn the napkin over.

5. Fold the right and left lower corners to the middle of the napkin.

6. Grab the napkin from the point where the corners meet. Pull out the lower corner, the right corner, and the left corner.

# Water Lily, Graduated in Color

*A beautiful blossom on every plate — thus the banquet will start in a harmonious mood. You can also place a small piece of baguette in the middle of every blossom.*

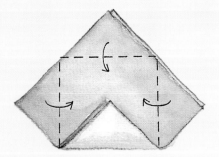  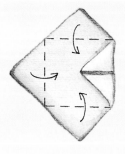

1. Place a green napkin on top of a beige one. The shape should be a diamond. Fold all corners towards the middle.

2. The napkin should now look like a square. Fold all corners towards the middle. Turn the napkin over.

3. Fold over all corners towards the middle.

4. Push with your thumb on the corners lying in the middle. Pull out the four corners lying underneath.

# Lotus Blossom with Leaves

*You can also use the gorgeous lotus flower as a decoration on a buffet or table — a figure fascinating and simple.*

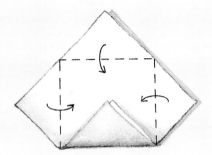

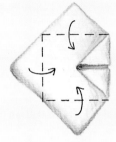

1. Place white napkin on top of a pink napkin as shown. Fold all corners to the middle.

2. Turn napkin around as shown. Fold all corners to the middle. Turn the napkin over.

3. Fold all corners towards the middle.

4. Push on the corners lying in the middle. Pull out the corners from the back side.

5. Hold down the corners in the middle. Pull out the corners lying between the four corners from the back side.

# Tips of Lotus Blossoms

*A figure in a class all by itself - but not difficult for trained banquet designers.*
*It is best to shape the tips of the lotus blossoms on the day before*
*the guests arrive.*

1. Place a pink napkin in a square. Place the green napkin over it shaped as a diamond, as shown.

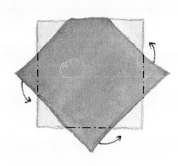

2. Fold the corners of the green napkin underneath the pink square.

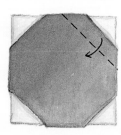

3. Fold the upper right corner of the pink napkin towards the middle.

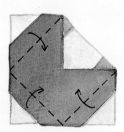

4. Fold all corners of the pink napkin towards the middle.

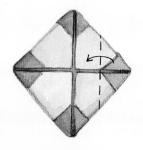

5. Fold the right corner towards the middle.

6. Fold all other corners towards the middle.

7. Turn the napkin over.

8. Fold all corners towards the middle.

9. Push on the corners lying in the middle. Pull up the corners on the upper right corner from the back side.

10. Pull up all other corners.

11. Underneath the lotus blossom are four "leaves." Each one is in between the "flowers." Pull each one out separately.

# First Communion/Confirmation

*A flat figure ideally suited for first communion or confirmation. It is very pretty if the ruffled ribbon harmonizes with the ruffles on the blouse or shirt of the young guest of honor.*

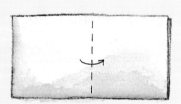

1. Start off with the napkin shaped as a square. Fold the napkin in half. Fold the halved napkin towards the right.

2. The opened corners point towards the upper right. Fold the top layer downwards over the diagonal.

3. Fold the corner now pointing downwards back up halfway. Then fold it down and up one more time.

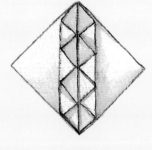

4. Fold the top layer in the right corner in the same manner as the last corner.

5. Turn the figure at a 45° degree angle to the right.

6. Turn the lower tip towards the back.

7. Turn the left and right corners to the back.

*Classic*

# Silverware Cover

*A flat figure that receives the flatware — ideally suited for a table outdoors, because the napkin is weighted down.*

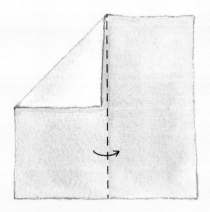

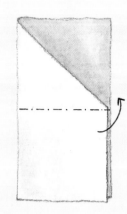

1. Fold upper left corner toward the middle. Fold the napkin to the right over the diagonal central axis.

2. Turn the lower half to the back.

3. Turn the napkin at an angle to the right so that the open side faces upwards.

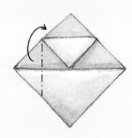

4. Fold the corners of the two upper layers towards the middle. Turn the left corner to the back.

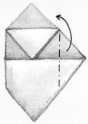

5. Fold the right corner to the back.

# Pro and Con

*One theme — two opposing points of view. This completely symmetrical figure
can be folded quickly and simply.*

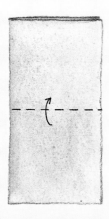

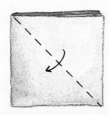

1. Place a light pink napkin over a dark pink one. Fold to the right. Then, fold the bottom to the top.

2. Fold the upper layer of the right corner diagonally towards the bottom.

3. Fold the upper layer of the lower left corner upwards, as shown.

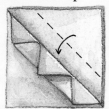

4. Fold the tip of the corner back again. Fold the other side the same way.

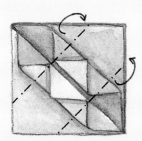

5. Fold the two corners backwards as illustrated.

# Napkin Pocket Book

*Your guests will be amazed at the handsome pocket book that is actually a napkin. And it will be real fun to find a small present inside.*

1. Fold the napkin to the left. Fold the lower part towards the top.

2. Fold the upper left corner towards the middle.

3. Fold the right upper corner towards the middle.

4. Fold both corners down.

5. Fold the next corners the same as the last corners.

6. Fold the corners down over the second triangle.

*Classic*

# Egyptian Felucca

*At a meal with napkins in the shape of an Egyptian felucca, serve Arabian or Middle Eastern delicacies. It will be an evening from "One Thousand and One Nights."*

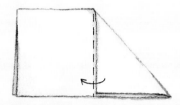

1. Fold the napkin in half. Fold the upper right corner into the middle.

2. Fold the right corner over the middle to the right.

3. Fold the right lower corner diagonally to the upper left.

4. Turn figure as shown.

5. Turn each of the four corners up, individually.

64

# Crusader

*At a rustic meal, a large napkin should not be absent. The sturdy figure of a
Crusader is ideal.*

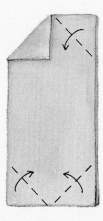

1 Fold the napkin in half. Then
fold each corner in towards the
middle.

2. Fold the lower triangle
upwards.

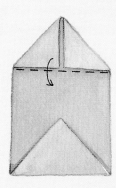

3. Fold the upper triangle
downwards.

4. Turn the napkin over. Fold
all corners towards the middle.

5. Turn the figure over. Fluff
the two corners so that they
are standing up.

# Original Soutane

*With the simple reserved line of the soutane one will underline the reflective atmosphere during a religious holiday.*

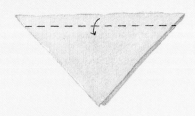

1. Fold the napkin into a triangle.

2. Fold the top down towards the center of the figure, as shown.

3. Fold the right corner downwards.

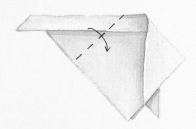

4. Fold the left corner downwards.

5. Smooth out the tips.

*Original*

# Original Shirt

*This surprise will certainly succeed. Fasten a brooch or tie tack for the birthday child to the flat figure.*

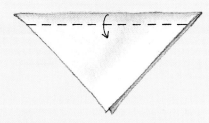

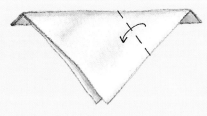

1. Place napkin with one corner pointing downwards. Fold diagonally in the middle. Fold the top piece downwards as shown.

2. Turn the napkin over.

3. Fold the right corner downwards.

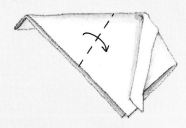

4. Fold the left corner downwards.

5. Straighten the tips in an exact symmetrical fashion.

*Original*

*Beautiful Napkin Folding*

# Original Hang Glider

*With this figure, you'll score points with your athletic friends. Hang gliders are a symbol of elegance.*

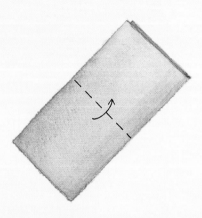

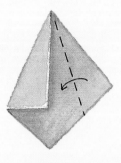

1. Put down napkin with one corner facing downwards, as shown. Fold in the middle to get a diamond shape.

2. Fold the left corner to the front.

3. Fold the right corner to the front.

4. Turn the napkin over. Fold the left and right corners to the front.

5. Pull out the corners to the left and to the right. Turn the figure over.

# Swan

*Very elegant and nicest on a opulent table. This napkin figure has probably
impressed you before. Now you will find out how to create it.*

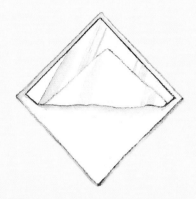
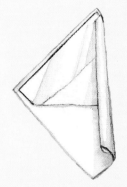
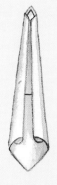

1. Put the napkin down with
one corner facing downwards.
Place a piece of foil on the
upper layer.

2. Roll up the napkin from the
right side towards the middle.

3. Roll it up from the left
towards the middle.

4. Fold the napkin downwards
horizontally just about in the
middle.

5. Fold the tip at the top diagonally upwards. This figure
combined with the "Sea
Urchin" will result in the
swan.

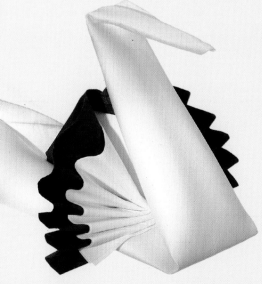

# Mountaintop

*A dizzying figure for all who assault peaks and want to reach the upper regions. The menu can be hearty as well as select.*

1. Fold the napkin vertically in half. Fold all corners towards the middle.

2. Fold the lower tip towards the top.

3. Fold the upper tip downwards.

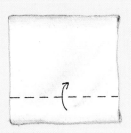

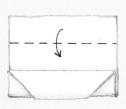

4. Turn the napkin over. Fold the lower quarter upwards.

5. Fold the upper quarter downwards.

6. Pull out the corner from below the upper edge. Pull out the corner from below the lower edge.

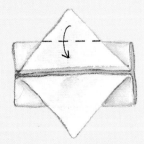

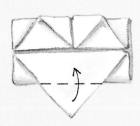

7. Fold the upper corner to the middle. Fold the lower corner to the front.

8. Fold the figure horizontally in the middle to the back.

9. Stand the figure up so that the three edges of the folds point upwards.

# Tropic of Capricorn

*We are at the southern half of the earth. Everything is upside down.*

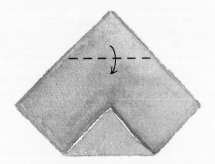

1. Place the napkin in a diamond shape. Fold the lower corner towards the middle. Fold the upper corner to the middle.

2. Fold all other corners towards the middle.

3. Turn the napkin over. Fold the upper left corner towards the middle.

4. Fold all corners towards the middle.

5. Turn the napkin over into a diamond shape.

6. Fold the upper corner towards the middle.

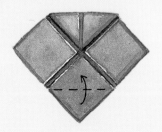

7. Fold the lower corner towards the middle.

8. Fold the right and left corners to the middle.

9. Pull out the upper right corner to the outside.

*Original*

10. Pull out the sides until the figure forms a rectangle shape.

11. Fold out all of the other corners in the same manner.

# Ice Cream Cone with Colored Ribbon

*Summertime is the time for ice cream. Just one look at an ice cream cone will cool off your guests. The flat figure will produce an original note on a colorfully arranged table.*

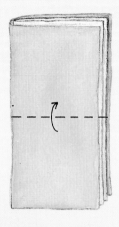

1. Place a beige–colored napkin on a yellow one. Fold in half vertically and then horizontally.

2. Fold the upper right corner of the yellow napkin as well as two layers of the beige napkin towards the middle.

3. Fold those three corners under themselves.

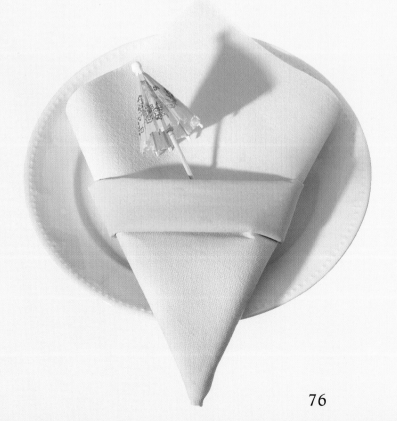

4. Fold the upper left–hand corner underneath the figure as shown above. Fold the bottom right–hand corner in the same manner.

# Colorful Surprise Bag

*This merry figure is a reminder of childhood. Do not disappoint your guests:*
*hide small, funny surprises inside the bag.*

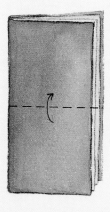

1. Place a yellow–colored napkin on a purple one. Fold in half vertically and then horizontally.

2. Fold the upper right corner of the purple napkin as well as two layers of the yellow napkin towards the middle.

3. Fold those three corners under themselves.

4. Fold the upper left–hand corner underneath the figure, as shown above. Do the same thing with the bottom right corner.

5. Fold the top blue corner underneath itself. Fold the bottom tip underneath the figure.

# Pocket Crab

*The gourmand knows immediately that seafood or a fish dinner will be on the menu. The pocket crab embellishes a sumptuously decorated table as well as a simply set table.*

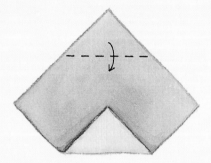

1. Place a salmon napkin on top of an apricot one to form a diamond shape. Fold the lower and upper corners to the middle.

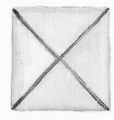

2. Fold all other corners to the center of the figure.

3. Turn the napkin over. Fold the upper left corner towards the center.

4. Fold all other corners to the center of the figure.

5. Turn the napkin over. Make sure that it is in a diamond shape.

6. Fold the upper corner toward the center.

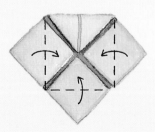

7. Fold all other corners towards the center.

8. Turn the figure over.

9. Pull out the upper right corner towards the outside.

10. If the shape is not naturally rounded, tug on its corners.

11. Pull out all of the other corners to get the final figure.

# Sandwich

*Even if only a little snack is to be served, a nicely folded napkin gives style to the small meal. With a bit of practice this napkin is easy to shape.*

1. Fold the napkin vertically in half. Fold all four corners to the center.

2. Fold the lower triangle upwards.

3. Fold the upper triangle downwards.

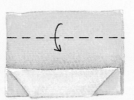

4. Turn the napkin over. Fold the lower quarter upwards. Fold the upper quarter downwards.

5. Turn the napkin over.

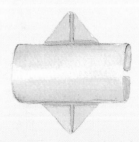

6. Turn the upper triangle to the outside. Turn the lower triangle to the outside.

# Sweden

*When having a dinner party with a Nordic menu, have a flotilla of*
*Scandinavian delicacies sail under the Swedish flag.*

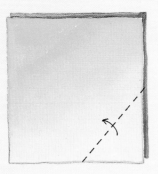

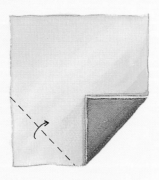

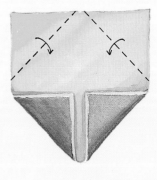

1. Put a yellow napkin on a blue napkin shaped as a square. Fold the right lower corner towards the center but not all the way to the middle of the napkin.

2. Fold the left lower corner towards the center but not up to the center of the napkin.

3. Do the same with the remaining two corners.

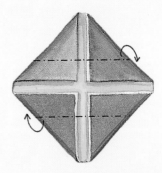

4. Fold the upper part of the napkin underneath the figure. Do the same with the lower part of the napkin.

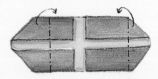

5. Fold the remaining two corners underneath the napkin.

*Original*

# Spain

*Memories of the vacation in Spain? Sharing slides of your vacation with friends at a paella? Then this figure will create the additional ambiance.*

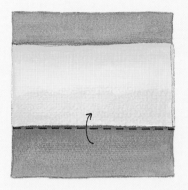

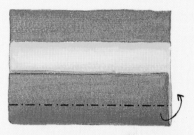

1. Fold yellow napkin in half, as shown.

2. Place yellow napkin on top of a red napkin, as shown. Fold lower red edge upwards.

3. At the bottom, fold one quarter of the red edge underneath the figure.

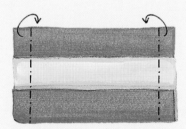

4. Fold the left side underneath the figure.

5. Do the same with the right side.

# Hourglass

*When the year is coming to an end, the hourglass reminds us how quickly time passes — a reflective figure for New Year's Eve.*

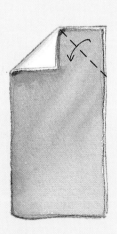

1. Fold white white napkin in half, as shown.

2. Fold a blue napkin in half, as shown.

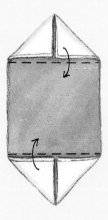

3. Place the blue napkin on top of the white napkin.

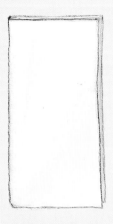

4. Fold the upper corners downwards.

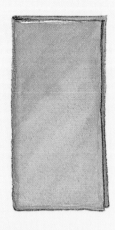

5. Fold lower corners upwards.

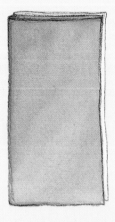

6. Fold the upper triangle to the center of the figure. Fold the lower triangle to the center of the figure.

84

*Original*

# Asian Fan with Lace

*An exclusive, very harmonious figure. This figure takes some practice to achieve. Place the figure in a vessel or stick it with the lower part into a napkin-holder made of glass.*

1. Fold a red napkin in half, as shown. At the bottom of the figure, fold the upper layer of the napkin towards the front.

2. Fold the back layer of the napkin underneath the figure.

3. Seen from the side, the napkin will now have an M-shape.

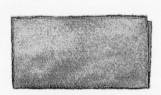

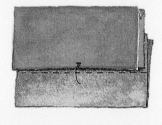

4. Fold a blue napkin in half.

5. Place the red napkin on top of the blue one. Fold the blue napkin over the lower edge of the red napkin towards the top.

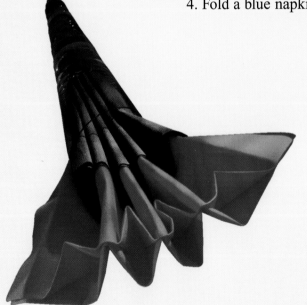

6. Starting on one side, fold into accordion pleats.

7. Hold the napkin together at the lower end.

8. Carefully fold the corners of the red napkin to face the outside of the figure. Turn the napkin around and fold the other corners to the outside.

9. Carefully fold the corners of the blue napkin to the outside. Finally, at the upper end, pull the figure apart.

# *Geisha Fan*

*Japanese dishes are always an exquisite visual delight. Set your table in style with a geisha fan.*

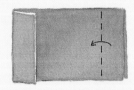

1. Fold the red napkin in half, so that the opening is at the bottom of the napkin. Starting at the left, fold about one sixth of the napkin towards the middle.

2. From the right, fold about one sixth of the basic shape to the left.

3. Turn the figure over.

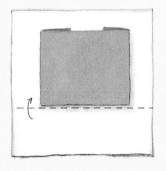

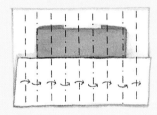

4. Place the red napkin on the upper part of a white napkin. Fold the lower half of the white napkin towards the center of the figure.

5. Starting at the left, fold the napkin into accordion pleats.

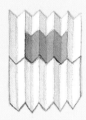

6. On top, pull the figure apart. Push the lower end together and decorate with a red ribbon.

# Blue Trout

*Are you having a fish dinner ? That is a good enough reason to serve blue trout.*

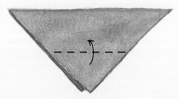

1. Fold the napkin into a triangle, as shown. Fold the lower corner up to the top of the triangle.

2. Fold part of the left overhanging triangle towards the front.

3. Fold the part of the right overhanging triangle towards the front.

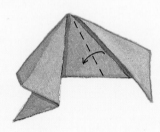

4. Fold the left half of the figure towards the center one more time. Do the same with the right side.

5. Turn the figure around. Decorate with a sea snail.

# Easter Rabbit

*No festive Easter Sunday meal should be without a bunny as a napkin figure.*
*A boiled egg fits into the yellow or brown Easter rabbit.*

1. Fold any napkin into a triangle which opens at the top. Roll in the triangle starting at the pointed tip.

2. Push the napkin downwards in the center to make a "V" shape.

3. Cross each end to make a circle for the hard–boiled egg.

4. With a ribbon, bind the ears above the rings.

# Smoking Jacket

*Let your evening at the opera or the theater end with a small dinner. The smoking jacket can be assembled quickly and looks festive.
Do not forget the candles.*

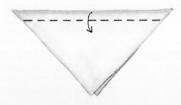

1. Fold the napkin into a triangle that opens at the bottom. Fold a piece of the top of the napkin towards the center, as shown.

2. Turn the napkin over.

3. Fold down the right corner, slanting slightly towards the middle.

4. Fold down the left corner, slanting slightly.

5. Fold the left and right corner underneath the figure.

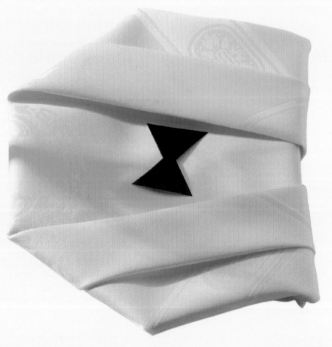

6. Fold the lower part underneath the figure. Attach a small bow tie of black cardboard.

# Flower Bouquet

*A picture perfect, colorful decoration for table and buffet. With such a greeting of welcome, every guest will be pleased.*

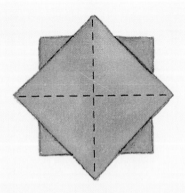

1. Place a green napkin on top of a red one, as shown. Lift in the middle and fluff.

2. Starting at the center, twist the napkins into a flower stem.

3. Bind the figure at the stem with a decorative ribbon.

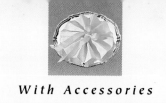
# Full Moon with Ribbon

*Catch the shiny moon with a decorative ribbon — the ideal figure for a harmonious meal for two.*

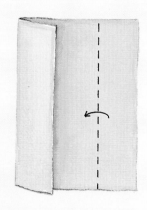

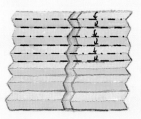

1. Fold the left quarter towards the middle.

2. Fold the right quarter towards the middle.

3. Fold the napkin into accordion pleats. Push the ribbon together in the middle and fasten with a ribbon.

# Acknowledgments

Photos: Angela Francisca Endress except for the following:

Archive for Art and History, Berlin, on:

Pg. 6–7: Auguste Renoir: *Breakfast of the Oarsmen*

Pg. 8 left: Johann Michael Voltz: *Lunch*

Pg. 8–9: William Pape: *Dinner at the Imperial Court*

Pg. 9–10 top: *Dinner*

Pg. 11: Louise Abbema: *Lunch in the Hothouse;*

Pg. 10 bottom: *The Decent Desire* supplied by Droemer Knauer Publishing

Pgs. 4–5, 12–13, and 16: Gisela Kelbert

Pg. 7 and all column vignettes pgs. 8–11: Falken Archive

Pg. 14: Photo Illustrations Ltd.

Pgs. 28, 32, 35, 37, 39, 65, 84: Tessmann & Endress

Pgs. 15, 17, 22 and all column vignettes

pgs. 14 to 25: TLC Foto-Studio

Pgs. 32 and 88: Michael Zorn

# Index